CW00664762

ECDL® 5.0

European Computer Driving Licence

Module 7b - Communication
using Windows Mail

Release ECDL260v1

Published by:

> CiA Training Ltd
> Business & Innovation Centre
> Sunderland Enterprise Park
> Sunderland SR5 2TA
> United Kingdom

> Tel: +44 (0) 191 549 5002
> Fax: +44 (0) 191 549 9005

> E-mail: info@ciatraining.co.uk
> Web: www.ciatraining.co.uk

> **ISBN-13: 978 1 86005 686 4**

The following information applies <u>only</u> to candidates in Ireland.

Acknowledgements:

> The European Computer Driving Licence is operated in Ireland by ICS Skills, the training and certification body of the Irish Computer Society.
> Candidates using this courseware should register online with ICS Skills through an approved ECDL Test Centre. Without a valid registration, and the allocation of a unique ICS Skills ID number or SkillsCard, no ECDL tests can be taken and no certificate, or any other form of recognition, can be given to a candidate.

> Other ECDL Foundation Certification programmes offered by ICS Skills include Equalskills, ECDL Advanced, ECDL WebStarter, ECDL ImageMaker, EUCIP and Certified Training Professional.

Contact:	ICS Skills
	Crescent Hall
	Mount Street Crescent
	Dublin 2
	Ireland

Website:	www.ics.ie/skills
Email:	*skills@ics.ie*

First published 2008

European Computer Driving Licence, ECDL, International Computer Driving Licence, ICDL, e-Citizen and related logos are all registered Trade Marks of The European Computer Driving Licence Foundation Limited ("ECDL Foundation").

CiA Training Ltd is an entity independent of ECDL Foundation and is not associated with ECDL Foundation in any manner. This courseware may be used to assist candidates to prepare for the ECDL Foundation Certification Programme as titled on the courseware. Neither ECDL Foundation nor **CiA Training Ltd** warrants that the use of this courseware publication will ensure passing of the tests for that ECDL Foundation Certification Programme. This courseware publication has been independently reviewed and approved by ECDL Foundation as covering the learning objectives for the ECDL Foundation Certification Programme.

Confirmation of this approval can be obtained by reviewing the Partners Page in the About Us Section of the website www.ecdl.org

The material contained in this courseware publication has not been reviewed for technical accuracy and does not guarantee that candidates will pass the test for the ECDL Foundation Certification Programme. Any and all assessment items and/or performance-based exercises contained in this courseware relate solely to this publication and do not constitute or imply certification by ECDL Foundation in respect of the ECDL Foundation Certification Programme or any other ECDL Foundation test. Irrespective of how the material contained in this courseware is deployed, for example in a learning management system (LMS) or a customised interface, nothing should suggest to the candidate that this material constitutes certification or can lead to certification through any other process than official ECDL Foundation certification testing.

For details on sitting a test for an ECDL Foundation certification programme, please contact your country's designated National Licensee or visit the ECDL Foundation's website at www.ecdl.org.

Candidates using this courseware must be registered with the National Operator before undertaking a test for an ECDL Foundation Certification Programme. Without a valid registration, the test(s) cannot be undertaken and no certificate, nor any other form of recognition, can be given to a candidate. Registration should be undertaken  with your country's designated National Licensee at an Approved Test Centre.

Downloading the Data Files

The data associated with these exercises must be downloaded from our website. Go to: *www.ciatraining.co.uk/data*. Follow the on screen instructions to download the appropriate data files.

By default, the data files will be downloaded to **Documents \ CIA DATA FILES \ ECDL**. Users of *Windows XP*, replace **Documents** with **My Documents**.

If you prefer, the data can be supplied on CD at an additional cost. Contact the Sales team at *info@ciatraining.co.uk*.

Aims

To demonstrate the ability to use an e-mail application on a personal computer. To create and send e-mail and to manage personal Contact Groups and message folders.

Objectives

After completing the guide the user will be able to:

- Understand what e-mail is and know some advantages and disadvantages of its use. Be aware of other communication options; be aware of network etiquette and security considerations when using e-mail

- Create, spell check and send e-mail. Reply to and forward e-mail, handle file attachments and print an e-mail

- Be aware of ways to enhance productivity when working with e-mail software. Organise and manage e-mail

Assessment of Knowledge

At the end of this guide is a section called the **Record of Achievement Matrix**. Before the guide is started it is recommended that the user complete the matrix to measure the level of current knowledge.

Tick boxes are provided for each feature. **1** is for no knowledge, **2** some knowledge and **3** is for competent.

After working through a section, complete the **Record of Achievement** matrix for that section and only when competent in all areas move on to the next section.

Contents

Section 1
Windows Mail

By the end of this Section you should be able to:

Understand Electronic Messaging and Related Issues

Use Online Help

Use e-mail

Change Screen Display

Close Windows Mail

To gain an understanding of the above features, work through the **Driving Lessons** in this **Section**.

For each **Driving Lesson**, read the **Park and Read** instructions, without touching the keyboard, then work through the numbered steps of the **Manoeuvres** on the computer. Complete the **Revision Exercise(s)** at the end of the section to test your knowledge.

Driving Lesson 1 - Using E-mail

P Park and Read

Today e-mail is an extremely important business tool and many businesses would almost come to a standstill without it. It has obvious advantages over the normal postal system: it is much faster - mail is delivered within seconds. Rather than pay excessive postage for sending paper copies of files through the post or by courier, electronic files can be attached to e-mail messages. All the sender pays is the cost of a local telephone call, or probably a lot less if they have a broadband connection. Consider how much more quickly business documents can be sent overseas using e-mail than by using surface or airmail. A point of note is that some anti-virus software/firewalls prevent certain types of attachment, which contain macros (such as databases) passing through. This is because some viruses use macros to work.

As it is possible to set up an e-mail account that is **web based**, rather than an account linked to a specific computer, messages can be collected and sent from any computer with an Internet connection, anywhere in the world. After having set up your account, it's a simple matter of logging on to send or read your messages. One disadvantage of web based accounts is that disk space is limited. This means that you need to keep an eye on the size of messages in your inbox; it can also prevent messages with large attachments getting through.

Before using e-mail, familiarise yourself with the rules of **netiquette** - network etiquette. Always use accurate and brief subjects in the appropriate field on a message. Keep your messages brief and relevant rather than rambling. Ask before sending large attachments; don't send heated messages (**flames**); don't use all UPPERCASE – it is the same as shouting; when replying, always make sure the subject is still relevant to your reply. Consider the implications very carefully before sending any sensitive information by e-mail. In a work situation, you must familiarise yourself with the e-mail policy in place. Usually, common business rules and regulations state that you must not send messages that might offend, or jokes, etc. Never send "chain letters". Basically only subject matter directly associated with the business should be sent via e-mail.

Make sure your outgoing messages are spelled correctly, just as you would before sending a letter. Many e-mail programs allow you to format messages with different colours, fonts and backgrounds. This provides an opportunity to show some individuality.

Unwanted Messages
Be prepared to receive unwanted e-mails. Certain companies and individuals send out masses of junk mail. You are shown later in the guide how to delete messages, so this should be useful. However, many of these types of messages have a link near the bottom that allows you to **unsubscribe**, so no further messages will be sent to you. It is always worth scanning the message for something like this.

Driving Lesson 1 - Continued

As was mentioned earlier in the Internet section, be vigilant about e-mail messages; they can contain viruses. Ensure you have up to date anti-virus software installed on your computer. Messages without a subject or from an unknown source should be treated with caution. <u>Save attached files to disk and scan them before opening if you are at all suspicious</u>. If you do open a message attachment that contains a virus, the results can be disastrous for your computer.

To send messages securely (encrypted), you can set them up to be signed digitally. A personal certificate is obtained by the individual to verify his identity and optionally encrypt transmissions. This is called a **digital signature**.

Any message, whether received via e-mail or through the door, which promises riches, prizes, or rewards in return for a cash payment or supplying your bank/credit card details should be regarded with the suspicion it deserves and be deleted or thrown away immediately. Some more subtle tricks have included official-looking e-mails supposedly from banks, etc., asking you to confirm card details and/or PIN numbers. This is known as **phishing**. Delete them. Banks will <u>never</u> ask for such information to be put in an e-mail. Be very careful who you give personal information to – **identity theft** is also a risk with e-mail. Take as much care to protect your privacy while using e-mail as you would in shredding normal mail before putting it in the bin.

On a slightly less serious level, false messages have appeared warning you that you have a virus on your computer and you must delete certain files to remove it. When you do this you find that your computer will no longer function.

Be suspicious of all e-mails from unknown sources. If in doubt, it is a good idea to get a second opinion. Preferably ask someone with experience of Internet and e-mail matters and whose opinion you trust.

Driving Lesson 2 - Using Windows Mail

🅿 Park and Read

For many people who are connected to the Internet, the majority of their online time is spent sending or receiving e-mail messages and there are many applications which will control this function on your computer. *Internet Explorer* comes complete with its own e-mail program.

Windows Mail is a simplified version of the messaging system used in *Microsoft Outlook* and is installed with *Internet Explorer*.

Windows Mail manages all electronic messages, both e-mail and newsgroup mail, coming to and going from the computer. Messages can easily be composed and sent to any e-mail address; files can be added to a message in a couple of steps.

If a user is not using *Windows Mail*, messages are stored for them until they are collected.

A very useful feature of the program is the **Contacts**, which stores information about contacts. If a contact's e-mail address is entered here, it saves the need for remembering addresses.

If a user wishes to subscribe to **Newsgroups**, *Windows Mail* can be configured to receive any newsgroup post. Newsgroup messages are sent in the same way as e-mail messages.

E-mail addresses

E-mail addresses are needed before a user can send or receive mail. An address consists of:

a **user name** -	the name of the mailbox where the server forwards incoming mail.
an **@ sign** -	separates the user name from the domain name.
a **host name** -	the address of the computer which sends and receives mail.

☞ Manoeuvres

1. To start *Windows Mail*, click the **Start** button, then **All Programs** and finally **Windows Mail**.

ℹ *Windows Mail must be configured before it can be used for the first time. Configuring is simply the term used to describe the supply of user information to the server, who "manages" the mail. Once the required information has been supplied, e-mail can be used. If the **Internet Connection Wizard** starts, contact your IT Administrator, who will be able to configure Windows Mail.*

Driving Lesson 2 - Continued

2.   If you are using a dial up connection a dialog box may be displayed informing that you are working offline and asks to connect - do it (this step does not apply if you are using a broadband connection).

3.   *Windows Mail* automatically opens the e-mail inbox folder. Double click the welcome message (if present). It opens in a new window.

The welcome message will only be present when **Windows Mail** *is first started. There may be other messages in your* **Inbox***, or it may be empty.*

4.   Read and then close the message by clicking ▣.

5.   Leave the main *Windows Mail* window open for the next Driving Lesson.

Driving Lesson 3 - E-mail Help

▣ Park and Read

Windows Mail contains an online **Help** facility that may assist when certain problems are experienced.

⌖ Manoeuvres

1. Select **Help | View Help**.

2. Connect to the *Internet* if prompted. **Windows Help and Support** opens, displaying a help window.

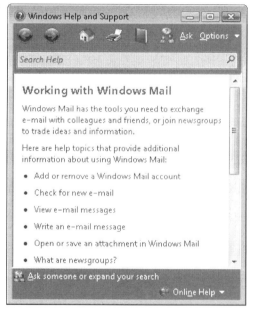

3. Click on one of the listed topics, e.g. **What are newsgroups?**, to display relevant help text in the window, then use the **Back** button, [⬅], to return to the main help screen.

4. There is an alternative method for searching help using **Contents**. Click the **Browse Help** button, [📖]. This screen displays a list of contents and works in exactly the same way using hyperlinked text to display the required information.

5. Click **Working with Windows Mail**. From the topics list click **Check for new e-mail**. The required help is displayed.

6. Type **virus** into the **search help** box at the top of the window and press **<Enter>**.

7. A list of topics relevant to your search is displayed. Click on **How can I tell if my computer has a virus?** The relevant help text is displayed.

8. Close the **Help and Support** dialog box.

9. Leave *Windows Mail* open.

Driving Lesson 4 - Changing Screen Display

P **Park and Read**

Windows Mail has a **Folders List** at the left of the screen, which contains a list of the various folders available, e.g. **Inbox**, **Sent Items**, etc. The display changes depending on the folder selected. It is also possible to change the main screen **View**, e.g. whether to preview messages before opening or not, or whether to display the list of folders permanently.

Manoeuvres

1. If an **Inbox** screen similar to that shown below is not displayed, click the **Inbox** folder in the **Folders Pane** at the left of the screen to display it.

2. Look at the top pane at the right of the screen. Messages in **bold** type have not been read yet. Those messages which are <u>not</u> bold have been read. Notice the icons to the left of the messages.

3. Click on the other folder icons, then select the **Inbox** again.

4. To see only messages which have not been read, select **View | Current View | Hide Read Messages**.

5. Select **View | Layout** to display the **Window Layout Properties** dialog box. Screen display can be changed from here.

Driving Lesson 4 - Continued

6. To remove the toolbar, remove the check from the **Toolbar** check box and click **OK**. The toolbar disappears.

7. Display the dialog box again.

8. Check **Toolbar** again, but <u>don't</u> click **OK** yet.

9. Normally, the contents of messages in the **Inbox** are previewed in their own pane below or alongside the message list. To hide this **Preview Pane**, remove the check from **Show preview pane** in the **Preview Pane** area of the dialog box.

10. Click **OK** to apply the new settings.

11. Select **View | Layout** and replace the **Preview Pane** in the correct position, then click **OK**.

12. Select **View | Layout** and click the **Customize Toolbar** button.

13. There are options here to change which buttons appear on the toolbar and to change their appearance. Look at the options, click the **Close** button and then click **Cancel** to return to the **Inbox**.

14. Select **View | Current View | Show All Messages** to make sure that all messages, read and unread, are shown in the **Inbox**.

Driving Lesson 5 - Message Headings

▣ Park and Read

The display of message headings in the **Inbox** can be changed to suit the user.

☞ Manoeuvres

1. To see the available column headings, select **View | Columns**. The **Columns** dialog box appears.

2. The currently displayed headings are indicated by a check in the box to the left of the name. Scroll down the list to see which other headings can be displayed.

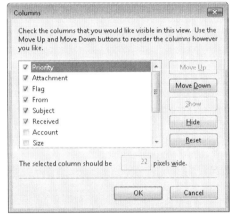

3. Check the **Size** box and click **OK**. Notice how the message heading **Size** now appears beside the others.

4. Select **View | Columns** again and click in the **Size** box to remove the check.

5. Click **OK** and notice how the message heading has been removed.

6. Select **View | Columns** again.

7. To make the date received appear as the first column, click on the word, not the check box, **Received** (this is the date an e-mail is received).

8. Click the **Move Up** button, [Move Up] until it is at the top of the list.

9. Click **OK** and notice how the message heading has moved in the **Inbox**.

10. To replace the heading in its original location, select **View | Columns** and make sure **Received** is highlighted.

11. Click **Move Down**, [Move Down] until **Received** is beneath **Subject**.

12. Remove the following message headings: **From**, **Subject**, **Received** and click **OK**.

13. Select **View | Columns** again and replace the headings.

Driving Lesson 6 - Closing Windows Mail

▣ Park and Read

Windows Mail can be closed at any time. With a dial up connection make sure the Internet connection is also terminated, if no prompt to disconnect appears. Whilst *Windows Mail* is disconnected, incoming messages will continue to be received and held, either by your mail service provider or your server. When you next connect, all waiting messages will be passed to your **Inbox**.

↷ Manoeuvres

1. Click the **Close** button, ▦, on the **Menu Bar** at the top right of the screen.

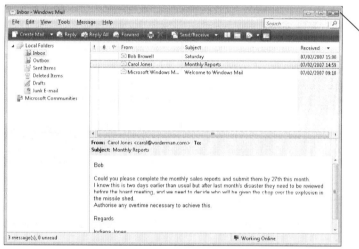

Alternatively, select **File | Exit** from the menu.

2. If you have a dial up connection the **Auto Disconnect** dialog box should appear. Select **Disconnect Now** to end the current session.

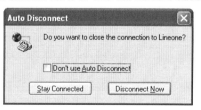

3. For dial up connections <u>only</u>, if the **Auto Disconnect** dialog box is not displayed, double click the **Connection** icon, ▦ in the **Taskbar** and click **Disconnect**.

Driving Lesson 7 - Revision

This covers the features introduced in this section. Try not to refer to the preceding Driving Lessons while completing it.

1. List some advantages of using e-mail in a business environment.

2. What is **netiquette**?

3. What can gain access to your computer via e-mail messages?

4. What can you do to protect your computer?

5. What is e-mail?

6. What are the three sections of an e-mail address?

7. Start *Windows Mail*.

8. Hide the **Toolbar** and the **Preview Pane**.

9. Replace the screen elements in their original positions.

10. Close *Windows Mail*.

i *Check the answers at the back of the guide.*

If you experienced any difficulty completing the Revision, refer back to the Driving Lessons in this section. Then redo the Revision.

Driving Lesson 8 - Revision

This covers the features introduced in this section. Try not to refer to the preceding Driving Lessons while completing it.

1.   Open *Windows Mail*.

2.   View the **Columns** dialog box and note the order of the currently selected columns.

3.   Remove all message headings.

4.   View only the following headings in the order stated: **Attachment**, **Flag**, **Priority**, **From**, **Received**, **Subject**.

5.   Reorder the message headings as follows: **Attachment**, **Flag**, **Priority**, **From**, **Subject**, **Received**.

6.   Reset the column headings to their original settings.

7.   Close *Windows Mail*.

If you experienced any difficulty completing the Revision, refer back to the Driving Lessons in this section. Then redo the Revision.

Once you are confident with the features, complete the Record of Achievement Matrix referring to the section at the end of the guide. Only when competent move on to the next Section.

Section 2
Message Editing

By the end of this Section you should be able to:

Create a Message

Insert and Delete Text

Cut, Copy and Paste Messages

Cut and Paste from Word

Use the Spell Checker

Add an AutoSignature to a Message

To gain an understanding of the above features, work through the **Driving Lessons** in this **Section**.

For each **Driving Lesson**, read the **Park and Read** instructions, without touching the keyboard, then work through the numbered steps of the **Manoeuvres** on the computer. Complete the **Revision Exercise(s)** at the end of the section to test your knowledge.

Driving Lesson 9 - Creating a Message

▣ Park and Read

Windows Mail allows the user to send an e-mail message to anyone on the Internet, as long as his or her address is known.

↱ Manoeuvres

1.   Start *Windows Mail* and select the command **Message | New Message**. The **New Message** window is displayed.

i *The* **Create Mail** *button,* 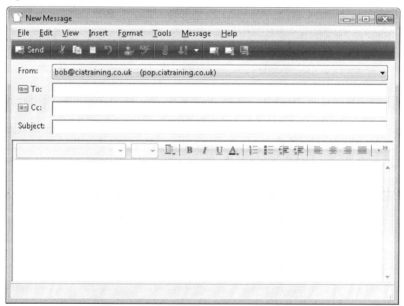 *, can also be used to display the* **New Message** *window.*

2.   Type your own e-mail address in the **To** box.

3.   You may also have addresses listed in **Contacts** (see Driving Lesson 23). Click the **To** button, ⊞To:. Double click on any name from the list and click **OK**. The message is now addressed to two people.

4.   In the **Subject** box, enter **Sending messages**.

Driving Lesson 9 - Continued

5. Type in the following text in the main part of the window:

    Always remember to check your e-mail regularly!

6. Double click on the word **regularly** to select it, then press **<Delete>**. Insert the new text **at regular intervals throughout the day!**

ℹ *Methods for inserting, deleting and formatting text in Windows Mail are the same as in most word processing packages.*

7. Press **<Enter>** to start a new line and type **You don't want to miss important messages**.

8. Select the two sentences. You are going to change their formatting. Make sure both sentences remain selected as each of the following effects are applied. Click on the **Font** drop down arrow, `Arial ▼` and select **Comic Sans MS**.

9. With the text still selected, use the **Font Size** button, `10 ▼`, to change the text to **12pt**. Embolden the text by clicking the **Bold** button, `B`.

10. Change the text to bulleted points by clicking **Formatting Bullets**, `▤`.

11. Indent the bulleted list to the right by clicking **Increase Indentation**, `▤`.

12. Click **Decrease Indentation**, `▤`, to replace the bullets in their original position.

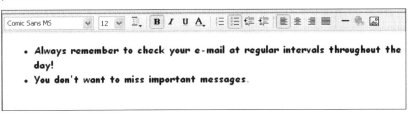

13. Use the alignment buttons, `▤ ▤ ▤`, to see the effect of changing the layout of the text.

14. Finally make sure the text is left aligned.

15. Leave the message open for the next Driving Lesson.

Driving Lesson 10 - Cut, Copy and Paste Messages

▣ Park and Read

It is possible to cut, copy and paste text to a different location within a message or to a different message entirely.

⌒ Manoeuvres

1. Using the e-mail created in the previous Driving Lesson, use click and drag to select all the sentences.

2. From the menu, select **Edit | Copy** or click 🗐 or press **<Ctrl C>**. The original text is left in the message, but a copy of it is now written to a temporary area of storage called the **Clipboard**.

3. Position the cursor at the end of the text, then press **<Enter>** to create a new line.

4. Select **Edit | Paste** or click ▤ or press **<Ctrl V>** to paste the copied text from the **Clipboard** into the message at the point where the cursor is flashing.

> **ⓘ** *Cut or copied text remains on the **Clipboard** until another item is cut or copied. It can be pasted as many times as desired.*

5. Now select the first sentence and select **Edit | Cut** or click ✂ or press **<Ctrl X>**. The text is removed from the message to the **Clipboard**.

6. Position the cursor at the end of the text and **Paste** in the cut text.

7. Click the **Create Mail** button, [✉ Create Mail] (or, if the button is not visible, select **Message | New**) and enter **Pasting** in the **Subject** box. The title bar of the message now shows **Pasting**.

8. With the cursor in the message area, paste the text. The text from the first message (**Sending Messages**) is pasted into the new message.

9. Click on the **Sending Messages** button on the **Taskbar** to redisplay the window.

10. At the end of the message type **Regards** and your name. Copy this new text and use the **Taskbar** to return to the **Pasting** message.

11. Paste in the copied text at the end of the **Pasting** message.

12. Close the **Pasting** message by clicking the **Close** button, [✕], at the right of its **Title Bar**. Select **No** if a prompt to save appears.

13. If the **Sending Messages** message is not already active, click on its button on the **Taskbar** to maximise it and close the message without saving.

Driving Lesson 11 - Cut, Copy and Paste from Word

Park and Read

It is possible to cut or copy text from a *Word* document and paste it into an e-mail message, so that time is not spent re-entering the same text. If the entire document was to be used in the message, it is more usual to attach the file. This will be discussed in **Section 3**.

Manoeuvres

1. Close *Windows Mail*, then start *Word* (**Start | All Programs | Microsoft Word**).

2. Type in the following text:

    To save myself time and money, I can use existing text in my Windows Mail messages.

3. Select the text and click copy in *Word* to copy the text.

4. Click the **Office** button, , and select to close *Word*. Do <u>not</u> save any changes.

5. Open *Windows Mail* and start a new message.

6. Click within the message box to place the cursor.

7. Click or press <**Ctrl V**> to paste in the text created in *Word*.

8. If necessary, insert a space at the end of the text and type:

    This text has been pasted in from a word processing application.

9. Click and drag to select **a word processing application**.

10. This text is to be deleted. Press <**Delete**> to remove it.

11. Replace the deleted text with **Microsoft Word**.

12. Close the message <u>without</u> saving.

Driving Lesson 12 - Spell Checker

▣ Park and Read

Windows Mail contains a spell-checking feature, which can be used to check spelling of all messages before they are sent. The spell checker is very similar to the one available in *Word* (though it is less powerful).

If none of the required applications are present this lesson can only be read for information.

☞ Manoeuvres

1. Create a new message with intentional spelling mistakes like the one in the diagram below.

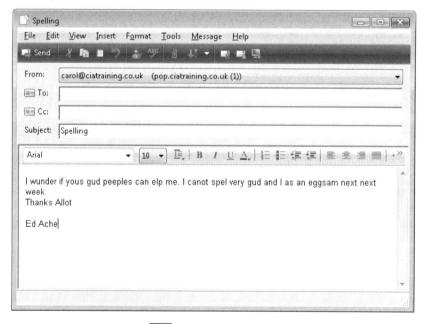

2. Click the **Spelling** button, , to check the message for errors.

3. When the **Spelling** dialog box appears, work through the errors found, either changing or ignoring them.

Driving Lesson 12 - Continued

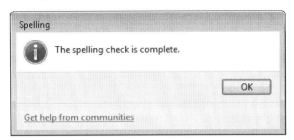

4. Click **OK** when the message appears to say the check is complete.

5. The **Spell Checker** may not be as good as those supplied with Word Processing applications, it does not detect the duplicated word - remove the extra **next**.

6. Some mistakes (allot for example) may not be marked as errors as they are correctly spelled words. Amend these words manually before closing the message without saving.

i *To have spelling checked automatically before each message is sent, select* **Tools | Options** *from the* **Windows Mail** *screen to display the* **Options** *dialog box, then select the* **Spelling** *tab. Check the* **Always check spelling before sending** *option and click* **OK***.*

7. Close the message <u>without</u> saving.

Driving Lesson 13 - Applying a Signature

▣ Park and Read

A personal signature can be added to the end of a message automatically, without the need for typing it each time. Several signatures can exist within *Windows Mail* and the appropriate one can be selected for each message.

☞ Manoeuvres

1. To create a signature, select **Tools | Options** and the **Signatures** tab.

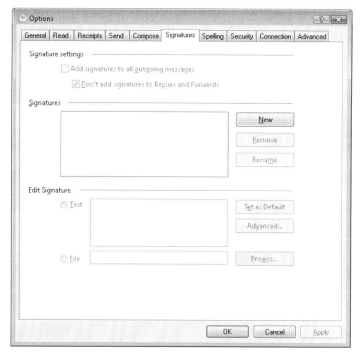

ℹ️ *If a signature already exists, e.g. if someone else has been using the same PC, you may wish to delete it by selecting it, then clicking **Remove**.*

2. Click the **New** button to create a new entry (**Signature #1** if this is the first one on the list).

3. Click **Rename** and change the signature name to something more meaningful, e.g. **Patrick's Full Title**.

Driving Lesson 13 - Continued

4. Enter the text desired in the **Edit Signature** area as shown in the following example.

 *To add this signature to every message, check **Add signatures to all outgoing messages** at the top of the dialog box.*

5. Click **OK**.

6. Start a new message. If **Add signatures to all outgoing messages** has been selected, the signature will already be present in the message area.

7. Enter any address in the **To** box and enter **Signature** as the **Subject**.

8. Type in a brief message. Add a blank line after the message.

9. To add a signature manually, select **Insert | Signature**. If there is more than one signature available, a list will be presented from which to make a selection.

10. Close the message <u>without</u> saving.

11. To delete the signature created, select **Tools | Options** and the **Signatures** tab.

12. Click on the unwanted signature to select it and click **Remove**.

 *The **Add signatures to all outgoing messages** option can be changed here if required.*

13. Click **OK** to close the **Options** dialog box.

Driving Lesson 14 - Revision

This covers the features introduced in this section. Try not to refer to the preceding Driving Lessons while completing it.

1.   Compose a new message and address it to a friend.

2.   Enter the subject as **Holiday**.

3.   Enter the following message:

> **Dear…**
>
> **I've just heard that you're going on holiday to Egypt and will be visiting the Valley of the Kings. Here's something that may interest you.**
>
> **Enjoy your holiday.**

4.   Press <**Enter**> and open *Word*. Open the **Kingtut** file from the **3 Word Processing** data files folder.

5.   Copy the first four paragraphs, then close *Word* <u>without</u> saving.

6.   Paste the text into the e-mail message.

7.   Delete the text **the "boy king", as he is often called,**.

8.   Cut **Enjoy your holiday.** from the original message text and paste it at the end of the message after the imported text.

9.   Spell check the message.

10.   Close the message <u>without</u> saving.

If you experienced any difficulty completing the Revision, refer back to the Driving Lessons in this section. Then redo the Revision.

Driving Lesson 15 - Revision

This covers the features introduced in this section. Try not to refer to the preceding Driving Lessons while completing it.

1.   Start a new message.

2.   Address it to a friend.

3.   The subject is **Viruses**.

4.   Enter this message:

> **I thought I should warn you that e-mail messages can contain viruses. Make sure your anti-virus software is up to date.**

5.   Create an informal signature for yourself.

6.   Add it to the message.

7.   Close the message <u>without</u> saving.

8.   Delete your signature from the **Options** dialog box.

If you experienced any difficulty completing the Revision, refer back to the Driving Lessons in this section. Then redo the Revision.

Once you are confident with the features, complete the Record of Achievement Matrix referring to the section at the end of the guide. Only when competent move on to the next Section.

Section 3
Send and Receive

By the end of this Section you should be able to:

Send, Open, Read and Flag Messages

Attach Files

Change Message Priority

Reply to and Forward Messages

Use Contacts

Add Sender to Contacts

Use Contact Groups

To gain an understanding of the above features, work through the **Driving Lessons** in this **Section**.

For each **Driving Lesson**, read the **Park and Read** instructions, without touching the keyboard, then work through the numbered steps of the **Manoeuvres** on the computer. Complete the **Revision Exercise(s)** at the end of the section to test your knowledge.

Driving Lesson 16 - Sending Messages

◫ Park and Read

Windows Mail allows the user to send an e-mail message to anyone on the Internet, as long as his or her address is known.

⬈ Manoeuvres

1. Click **⬛ Create Mail** to start a new message.

2. Enter your own e-mail address in the **To** box, so the message will come back to you and the results of this Driving Lesson can be observed.

3. In the **Subject** box, enter **Test message**.

4. A carbon copy of this message can be sent to another recipient who needs to take some action on it. Click in the **Cc** box and type in the e-mail address of a friend.

5. **Bcc** stands for **blind carbon copy**. To make this box available, select **View | All Headers** from the message menu. Use the **Bcc** box to send a copy of a message to someone who needs to know about the original message, but is not required to take any action on it. Other addressees are not aware if a blind carbon copy is sent. Enter a friend's e-mail address in the **Bcc** field (a different to the one in the previous step).

6. Type in the following message text:

    E-mail can be used to catch up with your friends, wherever they are, for the cost of a local telephone call.

7. Click **⬛ Send** to send the message to the **Outbox**. The message may be sent from here immediately.

8. If the **Outbox** still shows the message, send it to the server (where it is then forwarded to its destination), by clicking **⬛ Send/Receive ▼**. When this button is clicked, *Windows Mail* also checks for any incoming mail.

9. When the message has been sent, click on the **Sent Items** folder. A copy of the **Test message** is kept here, as are all sent messages.

> **ⓘ** *The options to send messages immediately and save copies in the **Sent Items** folders can be set or cleared by selecting **Tools | Options** and displaying the **Send** tab.*

> **ⓘ** *It can sometimes take a few minutes for messages to be received.*

10. Check with your friends that they received the message.

Driving Lesson 17 - Open and Read Messages

◨ Park and Read

Messages are received in the **Inbox** and are shown in bold type, with an unopened envelope icon next to the sender's information, ✉Gillian Atkinson. Once a message has been read, its icon changes to an opened envelope, ◁.

↱ Manoeuvres

1.   Click the **Send/Receive** button, [Send/Receive ▼] and a dialog box will briefly appear to say *Windows Mail* is checking for new messages.

2.   Watch the new messages appear in the message pane. There should be at least one message (**Test message**, sent to yourself earlier).

🛈 *If the message has not arrived, wait for a few minutes and try **Send and Receive** again.*

3.   To read a message, either click on it once, then view its contents by scrolling down the preview pane, or double click to see the whole message, including the sender's e-mail address. Click on the **Test message** and read its contents in the preview pane.

4.   Notice how the envelope icon is now open and the message is no longer in bold type. By default, messages are marked as read after a few seconds.

🛈 *This default time can be changed within **Tools | Options**, on the **Read** tab.*

5.   To mark the **Test message** as **Unread**, select it, then select **Edit | Mark as Unread**. The envelope icon changes to closed and the text to bold type.

6.   Use the menu command **Edit | Mark as Read** to mark the **Test message** as read.

7.   Read any other messages which are present.

8.   Double click on the **Test message** to open it in its own window.

9.   Close the message by clicking its **Close** button, ⊠.

Driving Lesson 18 - Flagging a Message

🅿 Park and Read

Once a message has been read it can be **flagged**. This is useful if further actions need to be carried out on the message, such as a follow up call, reply, etc.

👈 Manoeuvres

1. Select any message in the **Inbox**.

2. To flag the message, click in the **Flag** column for that message.

3. The flag icon appears at the left of the message.

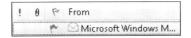

4. Select a second message from near the bottom of the **Inbox** list and to flag it by the alternative method click **Message** in the **Menu Bar**.

5. Select **Flag Message**. The item is then flagged.

6. With the flagged message selected, display the Message menu again. The **Flag Message** item is checked in the menu list.

7. To display the flagged messages together, click in the header of the flag column in the **Inbox**.

8. Remove the flag from each message in turn by clicking on the flag icon for each one.

Driving Lesson 19 - Attaching Files

▣ Park and Read

It is possible to attach any sort of file to an e-mail message *in Windows Mail,* provided it doesn't exceed the size the destination mailbox will allow (if this is the case the message will be returned undelivered). This makes it easy to send reports, charts, sound files or pictures, for example. When the message reaches its destination, the paperclip icon adjacent to the envelope, ⌀ ✉, will let the recipient know there is an attachment.

⟰ Manoeuvres

1. Within **Inbox**, click on the **Create Mail** button, ⬛ Create Mail .

2. Enter a friend's e-mail address (or your own) in the **To** box and enter the **Subject** as **Attachment**.

3. In the message area, type the following text:

    Could you look at the attached file and let me know which wines you want to order for the party next week?

4. Click the **Attach** button, 🔘 and the **Open** dialog box will appear.

5. Select the location where the ECDL word processing data files are stored (a folder named **3 Word Processing**), then double click on the **Winelist** file to attach it.

6. All attached files are listed in an **Attach** box which opens up in the message header area just under the **Subject** box.

7. To attach a second file, repeat steps **4** and **5**, this time double clicking the **Banking** file from the same location.

8. The **Banking** file has been attached in error. To delete this attachment, select its entry in the **Attach** box, then press **<Delete>**.

9. Click ⬛ Send , then ⬛ Send/Receive ▾ to send the message together with its attachment.

10. Leave *Windows Mail* open.

Driving Lesson 20 - Open and Save a File Attachment

 Park and Read

When a message with an attachment is received, it can be opened, saved, or both. You should be aware that some anti-virus protection and firewall software can prevent you receiving certain types of attachment. If you are connected to a network – in an office for example – it may also have been set up to prevent access to these types of attachment. Typically, problems may occur when receiving files with an **.exe** or **.mdb** extension. These files run scripts and macros in order to function – so do many types of virus. Attachments are a common way for viruses to be introduced to your system. Be very wary of opening any attachment if you are not absolutely sure of its source.

 __Windows Mail__ has certain security settings applied by default too. You can check the settings by selecting __Tools | Options__ and the __Security__ tab.When a message with an attachment is received, it can be opened, saved, or both.

Manoeuvres

1. Within **Inbox**, create a new message and enter your own e-mail address in the **To** box.

2. Enter the subject as **Saving Attachments**.

3. In the message area, type **The attached file may be of interest to you.**

4. Attach the **Maneaters** file from the ECDL word processing data files, as described in the previous Driving Lesson.

5. Click , then [Send/Receive ▼].

6. If necessary, wait a few seconds before clicking [Send/Receive ▼] again to receive the message.

[i] *It is possible that Windows Mail will identify this message as __Junk Mail__ and store it in a special __Junk E-mail__ folder. If so, open the __Junk E-mail__ folder from the __Folders Pane__ and either work in that folder, or select the __Saving Attachments__ message and click the __Not Junk__ button, [Not Junk]. The message will be moved to the __Inbox__.*

7. Double click on the message to open it. To open the attachment, double click on the icon in the **Attach** box of the message.

Driving Lesson 20 - Continued

8. For security reasons there will be a prompt dialog box asking for confirmation. Select **Open**. *Word* starts, displaying the contents of the attached file.

9. Close *Word* and the message.

10. To save the attachment, make sure the **Saving Attachments** message is opened or selected.

11. Select **File | Save Attachments**.

12. When the **Save Attachments** dialog box appears, ensure **Save To** shows **Documents**.

i *If **Documents** is not shown in the **Save To** box by default, use the **Browse** button to locate it.*

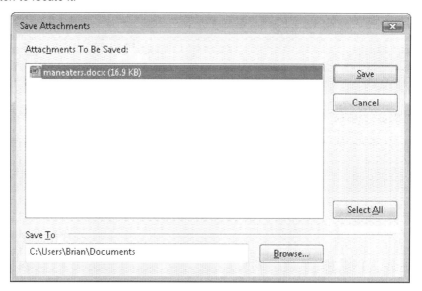

i *If more than one attachment is listed, select the required one(s) or click the **Select All** button.*

13. Click **Save** to save the attached file or files.

14. Open the **Documents** folder from the **Start** menu to see the file.

15. Close the **Documents** window.

Driving Lesson 21 - Changing Message Priority

🅿 Park and Read

Messages have **Normal** priority by default, but it is possible to change their priority to either **High** or **Low**. This does not mean that they are sent more quickly or slowly, only that the recipient will be aware of their urgency by an icon at the left of the message.

👉 Manoeuvres

1. Start a new message.

2. Address it to yourself and enter the subject as **Urgent!**

3. In the message area, type **Don't forget the meeting with the area manager at 2pm today.**

4. Click on the drop down arrow at the right of the **Set Priority** button and select **High Priority** from the list.

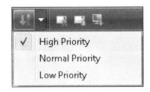

5. A bar appears across the top of the message to show that it is high priority.

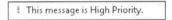

6. Send the message, then after a few seconds, click ![Send/Receive].

7. When the message arrives in the **Inbox**, look at the icon next to it. It should look like this: ![icon].

8. Mark the message as read, without opening it.

ℹ️ *The process to make a message low priority is the same. Select **Low Priority** from the button. The bar on the message will indicate that it is Low Priority, and it will have a low priority icon when it is received.*

Driving Lesson 22 - Reply to/Forward Messages

Park and Read

A user can reply to the sender of a message, or reply to all the recipients of a message as well as the original sender. A message form will appear where the reply can be entered (the original message will be underneath for reference). A message can also be forwarded to someone who wasn't on the original send list.

Manoeuvres

1. Within **Inbox**, select the message named **Urgent**.

2. Click on the **Reply** button, **Reply**, to display a message form, addressed to the sender of the original message. The original message is displayed.

The **Reply All** button is used to reply to all recipients of the original message.

3. If you do not want the original message to appear in <u>every</u> reply you send, it can be omitted automatically. Minimise the reply message window and from the **Inbox** select **Tools | Options** and the **Send** tab.

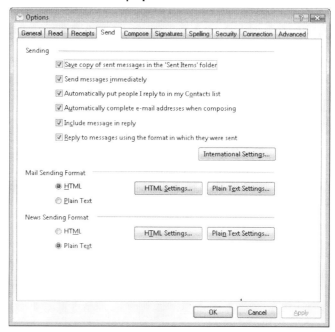

4. Remove the check from **Include message in reply** and click **OK**.

Driving Lesson 22 - Continued

5.   Maximise the **Urgent** message and close it <u>without</u> saving, if prompted.

6.   To see the effect of the new settings, click 🔄 Reply again. Notice how the original message is not included.

7.   The **Subject** section begins with **Re:** indicating a reply to a previous message. After **Re:**, delete the existing subject and replace it with **Replying to messages**.

8.   Enter the following message text:

     I was aware of the meeting. There is no need for concern, but thank you for your message.

9.   Click **Send**, then **Send and Receive**.

10. To change the settings to their usual status, select **Tools | Options** and the **Send** tab, then replace the check in **Include message in reply**. Click **OK** to confirm the change.

11. Select the **Urgent** message and click the **Reply** button. The original message can be deleted manually - use the mouse to highlight the text, then delete it. (This method is used to remove an original message from the current reply only).

12. Close the message window <u>without</u> saving.

13. Select the **Urgent** message again, then click the **Forward** button, 🔄 Forward. When the message form is displayed, click in **To** and enter a friend's address.

14. The **Subject** section begins with **Fw:** indicating a forward message. The forwarding message can be typed in the main window, leaving the original message underneath for reference. In the **Subject** box, enter **Forwarding messages**.

15. In the message area, enter the following text, above the original message:

     This message is forwarded as part of Module 7 of the ECDL.

16. Click **Send**, then **Send and Receive**. The message has been forwarded to a friend.

17. Leave *Windows Mail* open.

Driving Lesson 23 - Contacts

▣ Park and Read

To avoid typing addresses on to every e-mail message, it is good practice to create a **Contacts List**, which lists the details and e-mail addresses of contacts. This saves the trouble of typing e-mail addresses each time mail is sent.

⟰ Manoeuvres

1.   Click the **Contacts** button, , from the **Inbox** toolbar to display the **Contacts** window.

2.   Select **File | New | Contact**.

3.   Enter your own details in the relevant boxes (click **Add** after entering the **E-Mail Address**). Data can be entered under each of the tabs for information purposes, but only **Name and E-mail** tab data is required.

ℹ   *If a **Nickname** is entered, a message can be sent to this person by typing only their nickname in the **To** box of the message.*

4.   Click **OK**, then in the same way, add the names and details of four friends to the **Contacts**.

Name	E-mail Address	Business phone
Anton Haas.contact	anton@qromberg.com	
Bill Barnacle.contact	bill@ciatraining.co.uk	
Claude Chevalier.cont...	claude@LaTourap.com	
Seymour Sites.contact	seymour@ciatraining.co.uk	
Susan Jones.contact	sujo@hurnthax.co.uk	

5.   Close the **Contacts** window.

Driving Lesson 24 - Add Sender to Contacts

▣ Park and Read

When a message is received from a contact, there is a quick and easy way to add that contact's details to your address book.

↷ Manoeuvres

1. Right click on one of the messages in your **Inbox** to display the following shortcut menu.

2. Select **Add Sender to Contacts** from the shortcut menu.

3. Open the **Contacts** and scroll down the list to see the new entry.

ℹ️ *To automatically add addresses to which replies have been sent, to Contacts, select **Tools | Options | Send** and make sure there is a check next to the option **Automatically put people I reply to in my Contacts list**, then click **OK**.*

4. Close the **Contacts**.

5. The contact just added to the **Contacts** has decided to move to a desert island, with no forwarding address. Open the **Contacts** again.

6. Select the contact. To delete this mail address from the list, click the **Delete** button, 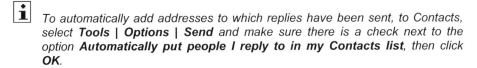, on the toolbar of the **Contacts**.

7. Click **Yes** at the prompt to delete the contact's details.

8. Close the **Contacts**, but leave the **Inbox** open.

Driving Lesson 25 - Contact Groups

▣ Park and Read

It is possible to create **Contact Groups** of specific contacts, so that messages can be sent to groups of people with a single click of the mouse. Multiple Contact Groups can be created, each containing particular types of contact, such as family, darts team, friends, etc. Any contact can belong to more than one list.

⟲ Manoeuvres

1.   To create a **Contact Group**, open **Contacts**. Click the **New Contact Group** button, [New Contact Group] to display the **Properties** dialog box.

2.   Enter **Friends** in the **Group Name** box. This is the name of the distribution list.

3.   Click **Add to Contact Group**. The **Contacts** folder is displayed. Select the first of your friends' names from the list and click **Add** to add them to the **Friends** list.

4.   Repeat the process to add other friends to the list. Multiple selections can be made using any technique then several records can be added at once.

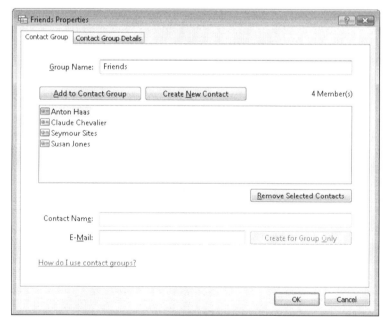

Driving Lesson 25 - Continued

5.   Click **OK** to close the **Properties** dialog box. The **Friends** group is now displayed in **Contacts**.

Name	E-mail Address	Business phone
Anton Haas.contact	anton@qromberg.com	
Bill Barnacle.contact	bill@ciatraining.co.uk	
Claude Chevalier.cont...	claude@LaTourap.com	
Friends.group		
Seymour Sites.contact	seymour@ciatraining.co.uk	
Susan Jones.contact	sujo@hurnthax.co.uk	

*Double click the group in the **Contacts** list to amend it or remove members. To remove a member from the list, highlight the name and click **Remove Selected Contacts**.*

6.   Close the **Contacts** window.

7.   Compose a new message. To send the message to everyone on the **Friends** contact group, click on ⬜To:. The **Friends** group appears with the other contacts.

8.   Double click on **Friends** from the list to add it to the **Message Recipients**, then click **OK**. The group name is added to the message

9.   The message will be sent to all friends who are included in the distribution list. Enter the subject as **Contact Groups**.

To:	Friends;
Cc:	
Subject:	Contact Groups

10.   Type in a suitable message and send it.

*To send the same message to several people in the Contacts who are not on a distribution list, click ⬜To:, then double click on each required name, before clicking **OK**.*

Driving Lesson 26 - Revision

This covers the features introduced in this section. Try not to refer to the preceding Driving Lessons while completing it.

1.   Check for any new messages in the **Inbox**.

2.   Read any that may have arrived.

3.   Select any single message that has been read and mark it as unread.

4.   Flag the selected message.

5.   Remove the flag.

6.   Close any open messages.

7.   Open the **Contacts** and add three new entries, using the names and addresses of colleagues.

8.   Create a new **Contact Group**, named **Colleagues** and add the new entries to it.

9.   Create a new message and address it to the **Colleagues** distribution list and enter the subject as **Diet**.

10.   Attach the file **Calories** (located in the **ECDL** subfolder **4 Spreadsheets**).

11.   Enter the message text as follows:

> **I thought this calorie counter might be useful for those of us starting the new wonder diet.**

12.   Make the message **High Priority** and send it.

If you experienced any difficulty completing the Revision, refer back to the Driving Lessons in this section. Then redo the Revision.

Driving Lesson 27 - Revision

This covers the features introduced in this section. Try not to refer to the preceding Driving Lessons while completing it.

1.   Start a new message and address it to yourself.

2.   Send a copy to a friend or colleague.

3.   Enter the **Subject** as **Web Page**.

4.   Attach the file **Images.htm** that was saved in the **Documents** folder as part of the Internet guide, Driving Lesson 33. If you do not have this file choose any other.

5.   Enter the body of the message as **Have a look at the web site in the attached file**.

6.   Send the message.

7.   After a minute check for incoming mail.

8.   When the **Web Page** message arrives save the attachment in **Documents**.

9.   Overwrite the original file if prompted, as the attachment is exactly the same.

If you experienced any difficulty completing the Revision, refer back to the Driving Lessons in this section. Then redo the Revision.

Driving Lesson 28 - Revision

This covers the features introduced in this section. Try not to refer to the preceding Driving Lessons while completing it.

1.   Create a distribution list named **Staff**.

2.   Add three friends or colleagues to the list.

3.   Create a new message.

4.   Address the message to the **Staff** distribution list.

5.   Send a carbon copy to yourself.

6.   Enter the **Subject** as **Team Building Trip**.

7.   Make the message high priority.

8.   Enter the following message:

> **This month's outing is to a local paint balling range. Please let me know if you are free on Friday week.**

9.   Send the message.

10.   Check for incoming mail.

11.   Flag the **Team Building Trip** message.

12.   Reply to the message, saying that you are free.

13.   Send the message.

If you experienced any difficulty completing the Revision, refer back to the Driving Lessons in this section. Then redo the Revision.

Once you are confident with the features, complete the Record of Achievement Matrix referring to the section at the end of the guide. Only when competent move on to the next Section.

Section 4
Message
Management

By the end of this Section you should be able to:

Save a Draft Message

Print Messages

Delete Messages

Organise Messages in Folders

To gain an understanding of the above features, work through the **Driving Lessons** in this **Section**.

For each **Driving Lesson**, read the **Park and Read** instructions, without touching the keyboard, then work through the numbered steps of the **Manoeuvres** on the computer. Complete the **Revision Exercise(s)** at the end of the section to test your knowledge.

Driving Lesson 29 - Save a Draft Message

▣ Park and Read

Occasionally, you may be in the middle of typing a message when you have to leave it, perhaps to check information. This doesn't mean the message is lost - you can save a draft copy and come back to it later.

↱ Manoeuvres

1. Within **Inbox**, start a new message with the subject **Meeting**.

2. Type in the message **Are you available for the staffing meeting on**.

3. You need to check the date of the meeting. Click the **Close** button on the message. The following prompt appears:

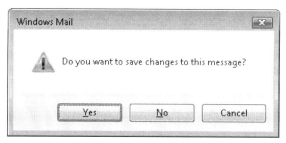

4. Click **Yes**. The information message shows it's been saved.

ℹ️ *Alternatively to save to **Drafts** select **File | Save** or press **<Ctrl S>** and then **Close** the message.*

5. Click **OK** if the above message is displayed.

6. Notice the **Drafts** icon, 📝 Drafts (1), in the **Folder List**, showing there is a single draft message.

ℹ️ *To continue a draft message at a later stage, click the **Drafts** folder. Double click on the message to open it and continue as usual.*

Driving Lesson 30 - Printing a Message

◼ Park and Read

Messages can be printed by simply opening the desired message, then selecting the print command. The number of copies and print range can be selected as required.

Manoeuvres

1. Within **Inbox**, open the e-mail **Urgent** by double clicking it.

2. Select **File | Print** or press **<Ctrl P>**. The **Print** dialog box is displayed.

3. Make sure the correct printer is selected. In **Number of** copies, use the up spinner to increase the number to **2**. Click **Print** to print two copies of the message.

4. Select the text **Don't forget the meeting** from the message area.

5. To print the selected text only, select **File | Print** and choose **Selection** from Page Range. Click **Print**.

6. Select a different message from the **Inbox**.

7. Click the 🖶 button and click **Print** in the **Print** dialog box to print one copy of the entire e-mail to the default printer.

8. Close the message, but leave the **Inbox** open.

Driving Lesson 31 - Deleting Messages

▣ Park and Read

All messages received are stored in the **Inbox**. After a period of time these messages will need to be deleted. Once selected, messages can be deleted and are moved from the **Inbox** to the **Deleted Items** folder, a temporary store, until confirmation of permanent deletion.

↱ Manoeuvres

1. In the **Inbox**, select the **Test message**.

ℹ *To select all messages, press <**Ctrl A**>; to select non adjacent messages hold the <**Ctrl**> key and click the required messages; to select a range, use the <**Shift**> key.*

2. Click the **Delete** button, 🗑, on the toolbar and the message is deleted.

3. Scroll down the **Folders List** and select 🗑 Deleted Items. The information viewer will now show all deleted messages.

4. To retrieve the **Test message** and replace it in the **Inbox**, right click on it, then select **Move to Folder**. From the list in the **Move** dialog box, double click on **Local Folders** and select **Inbox**, then click **OK**.

ℹ *A deleted message can also be clicked and dragged from where it is being vicwcd in the **Deleted Items** folder, to the required folder on the **Folders List**.*

5. View the **Inbox** folder to see that the message has been retrieved.

6. Delete the message again, but this time use the <**Delete**> key, which is an alternative method.

7. View the **Deleted Items** folder; the message has reappeared.

8. To empty the **Deleted Items** folder, right click 🗑 Deleted Items and select **Empty 'Deleted Items' Folder** from the menu.

9. In the **Warning message** box, select **Yes** and the messages will be permanently deleted.

Driving Lesson 32 - Creating Inbox Folders

◨ Park and Read

If the same computer is being used by several people, it may be a good idea to create a system of folders in which to store their individual messages. Once folders have been set up, messages can be sent directly to them on receipt. Messages can be moved between folders as required. Unwanted folders can be deleted.

᠓ Manoeuvres

1. To create your own mail folder within the **Inbox**, first make sure the **Inbox** is selected in the **Folders List** and then select **File | New | Folder**.

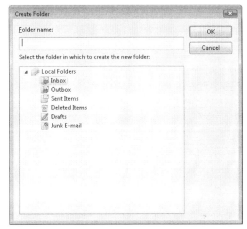

2. In the **Folder name** box, type in your first name and click **OK**. The new folder has been created.

3. The display in the **Folders List** changes to show the location of the new folder. If the structure within **Inbox** is ever hidden, click on the arrow at the left, ▷ 🔲 Inbox , to display it.

ⓘ *To delete a folder, right click on it and select **Delete**.*

Driving Lesson 32 - Continued

4. To arrange for incoming mail to be sent to the correct folder, select **Tools | Message Rules | Mail**. If there are no existing rules, the **New Mail Rule** dialog box will be displayed automatically

*If there are any existing rules, **Tools | Message Rules | Mail** will first display the **Message Rules** dialog box. Under the **Mail Rules** tab, click **New** to display the **New Mail Rule** dialog box.*

5. From section **1**, check the condition **Where the To line contains people** by clicking in the box.

6. From **2**, check the action **Move it to the specified folder** by clicking in the box. The dialog box should now look like the following diagram:

7. The **Rule Descriptions** in **3** can now be edited to show the correct name and folder. Click on **contains people**.

8. From the **Select People** dialog box, type your name and click **Add** (Alternatively select a name from the **Contacts**). Click **OK**.

9. Now click **specified** to select the folder to which incoming mail can be forwarded. Click on your folder. Click **OK**, then **OK** again to close the dialog box.

10. Click **OK** again to complete the process.

11. Test the rule by checking that messages for you are delivered to your designated folder.

12. Select **Tools | Message Rules | Mail** to display the **Message Rules** dialog box, select the rule just created and click **Remove**. Click **Yes** to confirm then click **OK** to close the dialog box.

Driving Lesson 33 - Organising Messages

▣ Park and Read

Once folders have been created, messages can be moved between them if necessary. It is also possible to sort messages in various ways.

☞ Manoeuvres

1. Make sure the **Inbox** is being viewed. To sort the messages by name of sender, click on the **From** heading at the top of the message pane.

2. To sort the messages by date and time received, click on the **Received** heading. The default order is to show the most recent first. This is useful as new messages will always appear at the top. Click the heading again to sort them in the reverse date order, then click again to restore the default order.

[i] *Messages can be sorted by **Priority**, **Attachment**, **Sender**, **Size** and **Subject** in the same way (ensure all message headings are displayed, see DL44).*

3. Select any message from the **Inbox**. To move it to your folder, first make sure that your folder is visible in the **Folders List**.

4. Right click on the message and select **Move to Folder** from the shortcut menu. Select your folder from the list in the **Move** dialog box and click **OK**. The message has been moved. Open your folder to check.

[i] *Messages can be moved to any folder on the **Folders List** by clicking and dragging.*

5. In the **Inbox**, sort all the messages by date received, with the most recently received messages at the top.

6. Select your folder in the **Folders List** and press <**Delete**>. A confirmation box is displayed.

7. Click **Yes** then expand the **Deleted Items** folder to show your folder.

8. Select your folder from within **Deleted Items** and press <**Delete**>. Another box is displayed to confirm the permanent deletion of the folder. Select **Yes** and the folder is removed from the computer.

Driving Lesson 34 - Finding Messages

▣ Park and Read

It is also possible to search for messages in various ways. For example, messages from a particular person, with a specific subject or content.

☞ Manoeuvres

1. To search for a particular message, view the **Inbox** and click the drop down arrow at the right of the **Find** button, .

2. Select **Message** from the list.

3. The **Find Message** dialog box appears. Read the various search options.

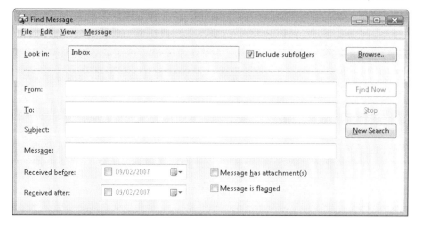

ℹ️ *It is possible to search for any messages that have been flagged by checking* **Message is flagged**, *or for any with attached files by checking* **Message has attachments**.

4. Enter your name in the **From** box, then click **Find Now**. After a few seconds, a list of messages received from you should appear at the bottom of the dialog box.

Driving Lesson 34 - Continued

i *If a consistent system of labelling **Subjects** on messages is used, it will be possible to search for all messages relating to a particular subject.*

5. Double click on a message to open it.

6. Close the message but leave the **Find Message** box open.

7. Click **New Search**.

8. This time, to search for a message with a specific subject, enter **messages** in the **Subject** box. This will search for any messages in the **Inbox** containing the word **messages** as the subject or part of the subject.

9. Click **Find Now**.

10. Notice the message(s) displayed at the bottom of the box.

11. Click **New Search**.

12. Click in the **Message** box. To find any messages containing text about the area manager, type **area manager**.

13. Click **Find Now**. There should be at least one message, with the subject **Urgent**.

14. Double click on the message to open it. Check for the text **area manager**.

15. Close the message and the **Find Message** dialog box.

Driving Lesson 35 - Revision

This covers the features introduced in this section. Try not to refer to the preceding Driving Lessons while completing it.

1.   Open the **Team Building Trip** message.

2.   Print three copies.

3.   Print the first sentence of the message text only.

4.   Close the message.

5.   Organise all messages in your **Inbox** by **Subject** in ascending alphabetical order.

6.   Print the first message in the list.

7.   Search for any messages in the **Inbox** with the message text containing the word **team**.

8.   Search for any messages with attachments.

9.   Search for any messages that have been flagged.

10. Close the **Find Message** dialog box.

11. Create a new folder in the **Inbox**, called **ECDL Module 7**.

12. Move all of the messages created during this module into the new folder.

13. Sort the messages by date received, with the most recent at the top of the list.

14. Search for any messages received from yourself.

15. Print these messages, then delete them.

16. Empty the **Deleted Items** folder.

17. Close *Windows Mail*.

If you experienced any difficulty completing the Revision, refer back to the Driving Lessons in this section. Then redo the Revision.

Once you are confident with the features, complete the Record of Achievement Matrix referring to the section at the end of the guide.

Answers

Driving Lesson 7

Step 1   E-mail is beneficial for businesses because it is very fast, cheap and web based accounts can be accessed from any computer with Internet access.

Step 2   **Netiquette** is network etiquette: a set of rules governing how you should use e-mail.

Step 3   Messages may contain viruses.

Step 4   Make sure you have up to date anti-virus software installed. Save attachments and scan them before opening if you are suspicious.

Step 5   E-mail is electronic mail.

Step 6   An e-mail address consists of a **user name**, an **@ sign** and a **domain name**.

Glossary

Address Bar	Shows the address of the page currently displayed in the Browser and allows entry of a new address to be visited.
Attachment	Any file transmitted with an e-mail.
Distribution List	A grouping of several mail addresses than can be accessed with a single name.
Folder	A method of grouping together files (and other folders).
Forward (a message)	Send a copy of an e-mail which you have received, to another address, with an optional message of your own.
Inbox	The default folder for storing all incoming e-mail messages.
Mail Rules	Definable rules on how to treat incoming e-mails depending on certain conditions.
Outbox	The folder for storing outgoing e-mails before they have been sent.
Preview Pane	An area of the **Inbox** display screen where the contents of messages can be viewed without opening them.
Recycle Bin	An area of storage where deleted files are held temporarily before being deleted completely.
Sent Items	The folder for storing outgoing e-mails after they have been sent.
Subfolder	A folder that is contained within another folder.

Index

Record of Achievement Matrix

This Matrix is to be used to measure your progress while working through the guide. This is a learning reinforcement process, you judge when you are competent.

Tick boxes are provided for each feature. 1 is for no knowledge, 2 some knowledge and 3 is for competent. A section is only complete when column 3 is completed for all parts of the section.

For details on sitting ECDL Examinations in your country please contact the local ECDL Licensee or visit the European Computer Driving Licence Foundation Limited web site at http://www.ecdl.org.

Tick the Relevant Boxes **1**:   No Knowledge   **2**: Some Knowledge   **3**: Competent

Section	No	Driving Lesson	1	2	3
1 Windows Mail	1	Using E-mail			
	2	Using Windows Mail			
	3	E-mail Help			
	4	Changing Screen Display			
	5	Message Headings			
	6	Closing Windows Mail			
2 Message Editing	9	Creating a Message			
	10	Cut, Copy and Paste Messages			
	11	Cut, Copy and Paste from Word			
	12	Spell Checker			
	13	Applying a Signature			
3 Send and Receive	16	Sending Messages			
	17	Open and Read Messages			
	18	Flagging a Message			
	19	Attaching Files			
	20	Open and Save a File Attachment			
	21	Changing Message Priority			
	22	Reply to / Forward Messages			
	23	Contacts			
	24	Add Sender to Contacts			
	25	Contact Groups			
4 Message Management	29	Save a Draft Message			
	30	Printing a Message			
	31	Deleting Messages			
	32	Creating Inbox Folders			
	33	Organising Messages			
	34	Finding Messages			

Other Products from CiA Training Ltd

CiA Training Ltd is a leading publishing company, which has consistently delivered the highest quality products since 1985. A wide range of flexible and easy to use self teach resources has been developed by CiA's experienced publishing team to aid the learning process. These include the following ECDL Foundation approved products at the time of publication of this product:

- **ECDL/ICDL Syllabus 5.0**

- **ECDL/ICDL Advanced Syllabus 2.0**

- **ECDL/ICDL Revision Series**

- **ECDL/ICDL Advanced Syllabus 2.0 Revision Series**

- **e-Citizen**

Previous syllabus versions also available - contact us for further details.

We hope you have enjoyed using our materials and would love to hear your opinions about them. If you'd like to give us some feedback, please go to:

www.ciatraining.co.uk/feedback.php

and let us know what you think.

New products are constantly being developed. For up to the minute information on our products, to view our full range, to find out more, or to be added to our mailing list, visit:

www.ciatraining.co.uk

Notes